THE 2000 ELECTIONS

Alan I. Abramowitz

With Introduction by Larry J. Sabato

Longman

New York San Francisco Boston
London Toronto Sydney Tokyo Singapore Madrid
Mexico City Munich Paris Cape Town Hong Kong Montreal

The 2008 Elections

Copyright © 2009 Pearson Education, Inc.

All rights reserved. No part of this publication may be reproduced, stored in a retrieval system, or transmitted, in any form or by any means, electronic, mechanical, photocopying, recording, or otherwise, without the prior written permission of the publisher. Printed in the United States.

Visit us at www.pearsonhighered.com

3 4 5 6 7 8 9 10 -V013- 13 12 11

Longman
is an imprint of

ISBN-13: 978-0-205-69291-0
ISBN-10: 0-205-69291-5

INTRODUCTION

In all of American history there has been no election for president like 2008.

The new diversity of twenty-first-century America burst through, and the citizenry was treated to the first African-American major-party nominee for the White House (Barack Obama), the first former prisoner-of-war to carry a party's presidential standard (John McCain), the first Republican woman to take her place on a major-party national ticket (Sarah Palin), another Democratic woman who nearly captured a major party nomination (Hillary Clinton), the first serious Hispanic candidate for president (Bill Richardson), and a dozen other contenders, all with their own special credentials and experiences.

Equally significant, young people throughout the country took a special interest in this election. Voters between 18 and 24 registered and voted at high rates, and they volunteered to do the necessary work of politics in unprecedented numbers—canvassing the streets, working the phones, attending rallies, and passing out literature. This powerful energy from a new generation has reinvigorated American politics, and the Obama administration may be able to harness it for even greater good.

If ever an election was worth studying and thinking about, it is this one. And in all of the United States, there is no one better equipped to analyze every aspect of the 2008 campaign than Professor Alan Abramowitz of Emory University. Dr. Abramowitz is perhaps the nation's foremost and most accurate forecaster of election results. He has been able to peer into the future a half-year or more in advance of an election to project the results with remarkable accuracy.

In this election update supplement, Dr. Abramowitz tells you everything you should know about this critical election. He reviews the political environment coming into the election year, the tumultuous presidential nominations that resulted in major upset winners in both major parties, the national conventions and the vice presidential candidates, and the course of the general election campaign.

Dr. Abramowitz's discourse on the November 4, 2008, results is fascinating. He covers the enthusiasm gap among party activists and volunteers that assisted Democrats and hobbled Republicans, the startling demographic and partisan shifts in the electorate, and the group voting patterns of race, gender, age, marital status, region, and religion.

The major changes in Congress are explained as well. Dr. Abramowitz shows how and why Democrats made substantial gains in both the Senate and the House—a result that will have implications for American government and politics for years to come.

This supplement reads as much like a suspenseful novel as a political science essay, because the election of 2008 was better than most novels. In fact, if 2008 were a novel, publishers would likely have rejected the manuscript because the plot was so incredible.

Real life can be like that, and this is real politics, 2008 style. Elections in America will never be the same again.

Professor Larry J. Sabato
Director, Center for Politics
University of Virginia

It was one of the most remarkable elections in American history. On November 4, 2008, Barack Obama, the son of a white mother from Kansas and a black father from Kenya, was elected to the nation's highest office. On his way to becoming the country's first African-American president, the first-term senator from Illinois had to overcome not just racial prejudice but persistent rumors that he was a Muslim and concerns about his lack of national experience. Before that, to win his party's nomination he had to overcome the enormous financial and organizational resources of the early favorite for the Democratic nomination, New York Senator and former First Lady Hillary Clinton, herself a pathbreaking candidate. But he did overcome all of these obstacles, and in so doing, made history. In addition to being the first African-American president, the 47-year-old Obama was the first non-southern Democrat to win the White House since John F. Kennedy in 1960 and the youngest candidate to win the presidency since Kennedy. Obama's victory was accompanied by major Democratic gains in the congressional elections. Democrats picked up at least 7 seats in the Senate and 20 seats in the House of Representatives, giving them their largest majorities in both chambers since 1995.

2008 was the first presidential election in over fifty years without an incumbent president or vice president on the ballot and the first in over thirty years without a candidate named Clinton or Bush on the ballot. On the Republican side, Arizona Senator John McCain, a party gadfly whose campaign appeared to be dead in the water a year before the election, overcame a field of high profile challengers and the opposition of many conservatives within his own party to secure the GOP nomination. McCain, who turned 72 shortly before Election Day, was the oldest major party candidate in American history. The gap of 25 years in age between the two major party nominees was also a record.

The 2008 presidential election sparked the interest of the American people like no other in the past forty years from the first caucuses and primaries in January all the way until Election Day. Over 130 million Americans cast ballots in the presidential election, an increase of 7 million over the 2004 figure of 123 million. The estimated turnout of 61 percent of eligible voters was one of the highest since World War II and the highest since the vote was extended to 18- to 20-year-olds in 1972. African-American turnout shattered all previous records. And Americans not only voted in record numbers in 2008, they also volunteered, displayed yard signs and bumper stickers, and donated money to the parties and candidates in record numbers.

It was a campaign full of twists and turns from Barack Obama's surprise victory in the Iowa caucuses to former New York mayor and early Republican front-runner Rudolph Giuliani's decision to skip the early caucuses and primaries and concentrate on Florida, Hillary Clinton's comeback victory in the New Hampshire primary, revelations of incendiary comments by Obama's former pastor Jeremiah Wright, Bill Clinton's attacks on Obama in South Carolina, Obama's strong showing in the Super Tuesday primaries and his subsequent victories in a series of primaries and caucuses that gave him a commanding lead in delegates, John McCain's decisive victory over former Massachusetts Governor Mitt Romney in Florida and his subsequent domination of Romney and former Arkansas governor and Baptist minister Mike Huckabee on Super Tuesday, a prolonged dispute between the Obama and Clinton campaigns over the seating of delegates from Florida and Michigan, McCain's selection of little-known Alaska governor Sarah Palin as his running-mate and a major financial crisis that forced both campaigns to react on the fly to a proposed 700 billion dollar federal bailout of some of the nation's largest banks. Through all of these twists and turns, however, the campaign was shaped by two dominant features of the political environment in 2008—a deteriorating economy and a deeply discontented but divided electorate.

The Political Environment in 2008

As the 2008 campaign progressed it became increasingly clear that the United States was experiencing its most serious economic crisis in decades. While it was a financial meltdown on Wall Street that brought the crisis to a head in mid-September, millions of ordinary Americans had been experiencing severe economic stress for months: unemployment had been rising and the real incomes of most Americans had been falling for well over a year. Underlying the crisis on Wall Street was the reality of falling home values and growing numbers of families facing foreclosure because they were unable to make their mortgage payments. The financial crisis served to reinforce the public's already overwhelmingly negative perceptions of economic conditions. According to the Gallup Poll, for example, between September 14 and September 24, the proportion of Americans rating economic conditions as excellent or good fell from 22 percent to 12 percent while the proportion rating economic conditions as poor rose from 40 percent to 55 percent.

Complicating the challenge posed by the increasingly dire condition of the economy was the fact that the man responsible for dealing with the crisis was one of the most unpopular presidents of the modern era. Even before September's financial meltdown, George Bush's approval ratings had been mired in the upper-twenties to low-thirties for many months. The president was so unpopular, in fact, that his own party took pains to ensure that neither he nor his equally unpopular vice president appeared in person at the Republican National Convention. Of course that did not stop Democrats from continually attempting to tie the Republican nominee to the man in the White House.

George Bush's low approval ratings were not the only sign of a deeply discontented electorate in 2008. Congress too was receiving record low approval ratings and overwhelming majorities of Americans were telling pollsters that the country was on the wrong track. The high level of discontent among the electorate was affecting the congressional elections as well, contributing to the decisions of 29 Republican House incumbents and five GOP Senate incumbents to retire rather than face potentially tough reelection battles with little prospect of their party regaining majority status. By retiring, these Republican incumbents increased the likelihood that their open seats would be taken over by Democrats. In contrast, only six Democratic House incumbents and one Democratic Senate incumbent chose to voluntarily give up their seats. And the toxic political environment for Republicans was also contributing to a large Democratic advantage in fund-raising in House and Senate elections. Not only were Democratic challengers and open-seat candidates raising considerably more money than Republican challengers and open-seat candidates, but the Democratic House and Senate campaign committees were also raising far more money than their Republican counterparts. As a result, the Democratic committees were able to provide much more assistance to their party's candidates in competitive races than the Republican committees.

But while there was growing sentiment that the country was in serious trouble and that major changes were needed, there was much less agreement about either the causes of the nation's problems or the types of changes that were needed. Americans remained deeply divided over foreign and domestic policy issues with Democrats and Republicans disagreeing sharply about what to do in Iraq and Afghanistan, how to deal with Iran, how to reform health care, whether to extend the Bush tax cuts, how to respond to global warming, whether to allow gays and lesbians to marry, and whether to restrict or expand women's access to abortion.

These disagreements were nothing new, of course. Partisan polarization had been growing in the United States since at least the 1980s. The conservative Democrats and liberal Republicans who exercised considerable influence in the U.S. Senate and House of Representatives during the 1950s and 1960s had become endangered species by the beginning of the twenty-first century. Almost all of them had died, retired, or switched parties. As a result, the parties in Congress were more ideologically distinctive and more internally unified than at any time since the New Deal era. And it wasn't just party leaders and office-holders who were moving apart. Partisan polarization was increasing among the public as well. Ordinary Democrats and Republicans were as divided in 2008 as at any time in recent history.

One of the most important consequences of growing partisan polarization over the past thirty years has been a significant increase in party loyalty and a marked decline in ticket splitting among voters. In recent presidential and congressional elections, Democratic and Republican identifiers, including independents leaning toward each party, have voted overwhelmingly for their own party's presidential and congressional candidates. As a result, the strongest predictor of the outcome of an election is the proportion of voters who identify with each party in a given constituency.

Given these trends, one of the most important developments in American politics between the 2004 and 2008 elections was an increasing Democratic advantage in party identification. According to annual data compiled by the Gallup Poll, between 2004 and 2008 the percentage of Democratic identifiers in the U.S. electorate increased from 34 percent to 36 percent while the percentage of Republican identifiers decreased from 34 percent to 28 percent. With leaning independents included, the shift was even larger: the percentage of Democrats increased from 48 percent to 52 percent while the percentage of Republicans decreased from 45 percent to 40 percent. Other polling organizations found very similar trends in party identification during this time period.

Gains in party identification were a major factor contributing to the Democratic takeover of the House and Senate in the 2006 midterm elections. According to the national exit polls, between 2004 and 2006 the balance of party identification among voters shifted from a one point Republican advantage to a three point Democratic advantage. The exit poll questionnaires did not include a question asking independents which party if any they leaned toward. However, the fact that 59 percent of independents in the 2006 national exit poll indicated that they had voted for a Democratic House candidate suggests that Democratic gains in party identification would have been even larger if leaning independents could have been included in the party totals.

The growing Democratic advantage in party identification meant that Barack Obama had a much easier task than John McCain in 2008. In order to win the election, Obama merely had to unify and energize the Democratic base; McCain, in contrast, had to not only unify and energize the Republican base, he also had to cut into Obama's support among weak and independent Democrats. Although he had overcome long odds merely to win his party's nomination, in the end the combination of a deepening economic crisis and a shrinking party base would prove an impossible burden for John McCain to overcome. But in order to understand the results of the 2008 presidential election, we have to go back well over a year to the spring and summer of 2007, when a large field of Democratic and Republican presidential candidates were taking their first steps on the road to the White House.

The Presidential Nominations: The Contenders

Without either an incumbent president or an incumbent vice president in the race—President Bush was constitutionally prohibited from seeking another term and Vice President Cheney had announced several years earlier that he would not run—a large field of field of contenders in both parties began jockeying for position early in 2007. By the end of the year, ten Republicans and eight Democrats, some famous and some obscure, had officially declared themselves candidates for their parties' presidential nominations.

On the Republican side, three members of the House of Representatives (Ron Paul of Texas, Tom Tancredo of Arizona, and Duncan Hunter of California) threw their hats into the ring even though no member of the House had been nominated for president in over a century. The rest of the field included three former governors (Tommy Thompson of Wisconsin, Mitt Romney of Massachusetts, and Mike Huckabee of Arkansas), two members of the U.S. Senate (Sam Brownback of Kansas and John McCain of Arizona) and one former member of that body (Fred Thompson of Tennessee), and the former mayor of New York City (Rudolph Giuliani).

As 2007 came to an end, there was no clear favorite for the Republican nomination. Although Giuliani, who was nationally known for his role in responding to the terrorist attack on New York on September 11, 2001, was the early leader in most national polls, many Republican and conservative activists were suspicious of his liberal views on social issues and his personal history, which included three marriages. McCain was a genuine American hero—the son and grandson of prominent admirals and a graduate of the Naval Academy who had spent five years in a North Vietnamese prison camp after his fighter plane was shot down in 1967. During his years in the "Hanoi Hilton," McCain was brutally tortured by his captors after he turned down an offer of early release. McCain enjoyed wide name recognition based on his unsuccessful campaign for the 2000 Republican presidential nomination but he was mistrusted by much of the GOP's conservative base for his past collaboration with Democrats and his relatively moderate voting record. In addition, his age—he would be 72 years old on Election Day—was also viewed as a problem by some party leaders and voters.

Mitt Romney had a picture-perfect family, a solid Republican lineage (his father had been a Republican governor of Michigan and presidential candidate) and a vast personal fortune that he could use to finance his campaign but his attempts to appeal to conservative Republican activists and voters were complicated by his moderate record as governor of Massachusetts, and his Mormon faith was viewed with suspicion by many of the evangelical Protestants who formed a large part of the GOP base, especially in the South. Brownback and Huckabee were both strong opponents of abortion rights and gay marriage, positions that appealed to a large segment of the Republican base, but both were little known outside of their home states and there was concern that they might split the vote of religious conservatives. Finally, there was Fred Thompson, who was probably better known for his acting roles than for his one term of service in the Senate. After delaying his decision for several months, Thompson finally entered the race in early September, hoping to unite the party's social and economic conservatives. But after an initial surge of excitement about his candidacy, Thompson's campaign was almost universally panned as disorganized and lackluster.

The situation on the Democratic side was very different. There New York senator and former First Lady Hillary Clinton was the clear early front-runner for the party's nomination. Clinton began the campaign with almost universal name recognition based on her eight years in the White House during which she transformed the role of First Lady by playing a prominent role as a policy advisor and spearheading the administration's unsuccessful health care reform effort during 1993 and 1994. She also had the advantage of instant access to her husband's extensive network of policy advisors, political strategists, and perhaps most importantly, campaign contributors and fund-raisers along with a large war chest left over from her successful Senate reelection campaign. Money was not expected to be a problem for Clinton's presidential campaign.

But despite the obvious advantages that she enjoyed, and her huge early lead in the polls, there were some early warning signs for Hillary Clinton's presidential campaign. While polls showed that she was well liked by Democratic voters, most of whom had fond memories of her husband's presidency, the same polls found that many Democrats had reservations about her performance as First Lady and about her ability to win a general election. These reservations provided an opening for other candidates to challenge Senator Clinton's status as the party's heir apparent.

Sensing an opportunity, seven other candidates eventually entered the contest for the Democratic presidential nomination. Former Alaska Senator Mike Gravel and Ohio Congressman Dennis Kucinich anchored the left end of the ideological spectrum in the Democratic field and provided some entertaining moments during the early debates but otherwise had little impact on the race. Based on their resumes, Delaware Senator Joseph Biden, Connecticut Senator Christopher Dodd, and New Mexico Governor Bill Richardson appeared to have strong credentials. Biden and Dodd had both served multiple terms in the Senate and played leadership roles on key economic and foreign policy committees, and Richardson, prior to his election as governor, had served in the House of Representatives and as UN ambassador and secretary of energy under President Clinton. But neither Dodd, who actually moved his family to Iowa so he could focus his campaign on that state's crucial caucuses, nor Biden, whose 1988 presidential campaign had collapsed after accusations that he had plagiarized portions of a campaign speech, were ever able to break out of the single digits in the polls. Richardson enjoyed a brief spurt of support in Iowa but quickly fell out of contention as well.

Even before the first votes were cast in Iowa and New Hampshire, two candidates had emerged as the main challengers to Hillary Clinton for the Democratic nomination: former North Carolina Senator and 2004 Democratic vice-presidential candidate John Edwards and Illinois Senator Barack Obama. Edwards's appeal was based largely on the name recognition that he had gained in his 2004 campaign, a charismatic personality, and a populist message that emphasized issues of poverty and inequality. But as a former senator, Edwards had no political base and his image as a champion of the disadvantaged had been somewhat tarnished by news reports about the multi-million dollar mansion that he had recently built for his family in North Carolina.

Obama, who was only in his first term in the Senate, had burst on the national political scene in 2004 with his widely hailed keynote address at the Democratic National Convention—an address in which he emphasized the need for national unity and criticized the bitter partisanship that had characterized American politics during both the Bush and Clinton presidencies. Along with his impressive rhetorical skills, of course, what made Barack Obama stand out in the Democratic field was his unusual background. Not only was Obama the offspring of a marriage between a white mother from Kansas and a black father from Kenya, but he had spent part of his childhood in Indonesia and, after graduating from Harvard Law School, worked as a community organizer in Chicago before being elected to the Illinois legislature. Obama's middle name, Hussein, was a constant reminder of his exotic heritage—a reminder that would be seized upon by some of his detractors to suggest that he was a Muslim and should not be considered entirely American. It remained to be seen how voters in overwhelmingly white states such as Iowa and New Hampshire would react to a candidate with such an unusual life story.

The Primary Calendars and Rules

The candidates in both parties had to plan their campaigns based on a schedule of primaries and caucuses that was not finalized until a few months before the first contests took place and complex sets of rules governing every aspect of the nominating process from how money could be raised and spent to how convention delegates would be awarded. The calendar was, of course, a key factor in shaping candidates' strategies. In contrast to a general election in which voting takes place at approximately the same time everywhere, primaries and caucuses are spread out over several months so that the results of earlier contests can affect the results of later contests. In 2008, the most salient features of the primary and caucus calendar were front-loading and compression.

Over the past several election cycles, a growing number of states have moved the date of their primary or caucus to earlier in the year in order to increase their influence in the nominating process. That is because state party leaders want to hold their primary or caucus before the nominations are settled so that candidates and the media will pay attention to their state. As a result, more and more states have been scheduling their primaries and caucuses as early in the year as party rules permit or, in a few cases, earlier than party rules permit.

Two states, Iowa and New Hampshire, have long played a special role in the presidential nominating process by virtue of holding the first delegate selection contests. In every recent presidential election year the Iowa caucuses have led off the nomination process followed a week or two later by the New Hampshire primary. Both states have had special exemptions from party rules that limit the time period during which states can hold their primaries and caucuses. More recently, in order to add a state with a more diverse demographic profile to the early contests, South Carolina has also been granted an exemption from the party rules and has held its primary shortly after New Hampshire.

Naturally, political leaders and citizens in Iowa, New Hampshire and South Carolina enjoy the tremendous attention that their states receive from the candidates and media by virtue of their states' special position in the nominating process. In fact, the New Hampshire secretary of state is required by law to move the date of the state's primary up as early as necessary to ensure that New Hampshire continues to hold the first primary of the presidential election. However, political leaders in other states, especially those with much larger populations, have long resented the disproportionate influence that these small states enjoy in the nominating process and in 2008 political leaders in two of those states, Florida and Michigan, decided to defy the national parties and schedule their states' primaries earlier than the rules permitted. The result was a prolonged controversy over whether to allow the delegates from Florida and Michigan to be seated—a controversy that was not resolved on the Democratic side until shortly before the party's convention.

With states competing for recognition and influence in the nominating process, there has been a steady increase over time in the number of states holding their primaries and caucuses on the first date permitted under party rules or shortly thereafter. In 2008, that date was February 5, which became known as Super Tuesday because of the number of primaries and caucuses scheduled for that day. A total of 22 Democratic primaries and caucuses and 21 Republican primaries and caucuses took place on Super Tuesday, a number that was unprecedented in the history of the presidential nominating process.

Although the last primary contests would not take place until June 5, fully four months after Super Tuesday, the fact that approximately two-fifths of the elected delegates in both parties would be chosen on February 5 led many observers to expect both party nominations to be effectively decided on that date. Ironically, though, because so many delegates would be chosen on February 5, the contests preceding that date, including not only the Iowa caucuses and New Hampshire and South Carolina primaries, but also the "illegal" Michigan and Florida primaries, loomed larger than ever because they would determine who had momentum going into Super Tuesday.

While the primary calendar was very similar for both parties, the rules for awarding delegates were very different for Democrats and Republicans and these differences had important consequences for the candidates' strategies and, ultimately, for the way the nomination contest played out in each party. The most important difference between the Republican and Democratic rules was that the Democratic rules required proportional allocation of delegates among all candidates receiving at least 15 percent of the vote in a state or congressional district, while the Republican rules allowed winner-take-all allocation of delegates. As a result, it was much easier for the front-runner to quickly accumulate delegates in the Republican primaries than in the Democratic primaries. In addition, under the Republican winner-take-all rules, winning a large state by a small margin was more advantageous than winning a small state by a large margin. However, under the Democratic proportional allocation rules, winning a small state by a large margin could be more advantageous than winning a large state by a small margin.

The second important difference between the Democratic and Republican rules involved the presence of party and elected officials at the two conventions. Under Democratic Party rules, approximately 15 percent of the delegate slots at the Democratic National Convention were reserved for party and elected officials known as "superdelegates." These superdelegates, including every Democratic governor and every Democratic member of Congress, could vote for any presidential candidate at the convention regardless of the results of the primary or caucuses in their state. In contrast, Republican rules did not provide automatic delegate slots for party and elected officials except for members of the Republican National Committee. Everyone else had to be chosen through the normal delegate selection procedures in each state. The presence of a large number of superdelegates at the Democratic National Convention reduced the chances that any candidate would be able to lock up a majority of delegates before the end of the primaries and added an additional element of uncertainty into the Democratic nomination race.

In 2008, as in every recent presidential election year, the Iowa caucuses and the New Hampshire primary kicked off the race for the presidential nomination. But in 2008 these contests took place earlier and closer together than ever—the Iowa caucuses on Thursday, January 3 and the New Hampshire primary only five days later on Tuesday, January 8. In between Iowa and New Hampshire, Wyoming held its Republican caucuses on January 5. After New Hampshire came a series of caucuses and primaries in January: the Michigan primary on January 15, the Nevada caucuses and South Carolina Republican primary on January 19, the South Carolina Democratic primary on January 26, and the Florida primary on January 29. Although Michigan and Florida had scheduled their primaries in violation of Republican and Democratic rules, the Republican National Committee had agreed to seat half of each state's delegation at the national convention, which left those states' primaries as the largest prizes available in the first month of voting. And Florida would loom even larger in the Republican race because it would take place only one week before Super Tuesday when more states than ever before would hold primaries and caucuses on a single date.

The Invisible Primary

Never before had so many primaries and caucuses taken place so early in the election year or so close together in time. As a result, candidates in both parties had to begin preparing for these contests earlier than ever by building organizations and campaigning in states holding early contests and most importantly by raising the large amounts of money that would be needed to compete in the early states, especially on Super Tuesday when the number and size of the states holding contests would require heavy spending on television advertising. This would require the candidates to make a crucial decision—

whether to accept federal matching funds in the primaries. Candidates who accepted federal matching funds could receive an infusion of taxpayer cash to supplement money that they raised themselves, but they would also have to abide by an overall spending limit and strict spending limits in each primary and caucus state. As a result, in 2008 as in other recent presidential elections, many of the top-tier candidates, including Republicans Mitt Romney, Rudolph Giuliani and John McCain and Democrats Hillary Clinton and Barack Obama, chose to turn down federal matching funds.

The phase of the presidential nomination campaign that takes place before the Iowa caucuses and New Hampshire primary is sometimes referred to as the invisible primary or the money primary because even before the first votes are cast and the first delegates are chosen, candidates begin to separate themselves in terms of organization and fund-raising. The 2008 campaign was no exception to this rule. The data displayed in Table 1 show that the invisible primary had clear winners and losers. In both parties, the candidates declining federal matching funds led the way in fund-raising and the amounts raised were unprecedented in the history of presidential nomination campaigns. On the Democratic side, Hillary Clinton's fund-raising prowess was no surprise. What was surprising, however, was Barack Obama's ability to match Clinton dollar for dollar in the early going. It was a clear indication that Obama's fund-raising machine, relying heavily on small contributions over the Internet, was a force to be reckoned with and would allow him to remain financially competitive with Clinton throughout the primary season.

Table 1. Total Primary Funds Raised by Presidential Candidates in 2007 (in Millions of Dollars)

Democrats		Republicans	
Clinton	98.7	Romney	90.1
Obama	99.6	Giuliani	56.1
Edwards	41.3	McCain	39.9
Richardson	22.8	Paul	28.2
Dodd	14.9	Thompson	21.8
Biden	10.2	Huckabee	9.0
Kucinich	3.9	Tancredo	8.3
Gravel	0.4	Brownback	4.4
		Hunter	2.5

Note: Totals include only funds eligible for use during primaries. Romney total includes 35.4 million dollars in personal loans.
Source: Campaign Finance Institute

The Early Contests

On January 3, the earliest date in the history of the Iowa caucuses, Democrats and Republicans in the Hawkeye State flocked to school cafeterias, church basements, and private homes to make their presidential selections. The results were a record-breaking turnout and a clear victory for Barack Obama on the Democratic side. John Edwards, who had devoted many days to campaigning in Iowa, finished second and Hillary Clinton came in third. It was a stunning setback for the Democratic front-runner and a dramatic breakthrough for Obama in a state with a tiny African American population. On the Republican side, Arkansas Governor Mike Huckabee capitalized on strong support from evangelical Christians who made up a majority of those attending the caucuses to score a decisive victory over Mitt Romney, even though Romney had enjoyed a huge spending advantage over Huckabee. Rudy Giuliani and John McCain had made little effort in the state and finished far behind the front-runners. They would wait for later contests in what they considered friendlier territory to make their first stands—McCain in New Hampshire and Giuliani in Florida.

Even though turnout for the caucuses was up dramatically over 2004, especially on the Democratic side, the approximately 230,000 Democrats and 120,000 Republicans who participated comprised less than 20 percent of Iowa's registered voters. In 2008, Iowa was one of a small group of states that still chose their convention delegates in party caucuses rather than primary elections. These caucuses have more in common with meetings than with ordinary elections. Caucus participants have to show up at a specific time and typically spend several hours sitting through the proceedings. Not surprisingly, turnout tends to be very low and after Iowa, media coverage tends to be sparse. But in 2008 the caucus states would play a key role in the battle between Hillary Clinton and Barack Obama for the Democratic nomination. In caucus state after caucus state, Obama capitalized on the greater enthusiasm of his supporters and superior organization to win overwhelming victories—victories that provided a large share of his ultimate margin in delegates.

On the Republican side, Mike Huckabee's victory in Iowa reflected his success in mobilizing conservative evangelicals and spelled trouble for Kansas Senator Sam Brownback who was trying to appeal to the same group. In a caucus state like Iowa a candidate with a highly motivated following like Huckabee had a significant advantage over candidates with less dedicated supporters. But it was not clear how Huckabee, an ordained Baptist minister, would fare in states like New Hampshire where evangelicals made up a much smaller share of the Republican electorate and where overall turnout would be much higher.

Voters in New Hampshire were accustomed to playing a crucial role in the presidential nominating process. For many years pundits and campaign strategists believed that winning the state's first-in-the-nation primary was a necessary condition for winning the presidency but in 1992 Bill Clinton managed to come back from a narrow loss in New Hampshire to win the Democratic nomination and the general election. Nevertheless, in 2008 most of the leading candidates in both parties spent many days trudging through the snows of New Hampshire in search of momentum heading into South Carolina, Florida, and Super Tuesday. When the results were tabulated they showed a narrow victory for Hillary Clinton over Barack Obama in the Democratic primary with John Edwards a distant third. The Republican contest produced a decisive win for John McCain over Mitt Romney with the other candidates trailing far behind. The other notable result from New Hampshire was the turnout which was up dramatically in the Democratic primary compared with 2000 and 2004 but down slightly in the Republican primary compared with the most recent GOP contest in 2000.

Clinton's comeback victory after trailing Obama in all of the New Hampshire polls following her defeat in Iowa reinforced the perception that the battle for the Democratic nomination was quickly becoming a two-person contest—a contest that would go until at least Super Tuesday. On the Republican side, John McCain's win over Mitt Romney, who was well known in New Hampshire from his years as governor of neighboring Massachusetts, who had led in the New Hampshire polls for months, and who had spent far more money than any other candidate, shook up the Republican race. Within days after his victory in New Hampshire, McCain, whose campaign had been widely viewed as comatose in late 2007, had emerged as the leader in national polls of Republican voters. Romney, who had been counting on victories in Iowa and New Hampshire to solidify his position as the GOP front-runner, and Rudy Giuliani, who chose to skip both Iowa and New Hampshire after disappointing polling results in both states, now faced a crucial test against a reinvigorated John McCain in Florida. But first Mike Huckabee, who had finished a distant third in New Hampshire, faced a crucial test of his own against both John McCain and Fred Thompson in South Carolina, the first southern primary.

South Carolina was a relative newcomer to the early primary season, added to provide both regional and racial balance, and in 2008, the Palmetto state would play a crucial role in both nomination contests. On the Democratic side South Carolina's large African-American population would provide the first test of support for Hillary Clinton and Barack Obama among this crucial Democratic constituency. John Edwards, a native South Carolinian, also needed a strong showing in the state that gave him his only primary victory in 2004 to justify staying in the race. Meanwhile, the Republican primary would provide a crucial test of John McCain's appeal in a state with a much more conservative GOP electorate than New Hampshire. South Carolina also loomed large for Mike Huckabee because of the state's large evangelical population, and Fred Thompson, who needed to demonstrate his vote-getting ability somewhere.

The Republican and Democratic primaries took place on consecutive Saturdays, January 19 and 26, and produced some dramatic results. In the Republican primary, John McCain scored a narrow win over Mike Huckabee with Fred Thompson and Mitt Romney finishing far behind in third and fourth place. McCain's victory in a state where he had suffered a crushing defeat at the hands of George Bush in 2000 reinforced his newfound position as the front-runner for the Republican nomination. Thompson, despite finishing a distant third, did have a major impact on the race. By cutting into Mike Huckabee's support among conservative evangelicals, he effectively handed the primary to John McCain.

One week later Barack Obama scored a huge win over Hillary Clinton based on overwhelming support from African-American voters who made up a majority of those participating in the Democratic primary. The results in South Carolina demonstrated that Clinton's support among African-American voters was rapidly collapsing in the face of Obama's emergence as a viable contender for the Democratic nomination. She would have to adjust her strategy in future primaries to take this new reality into account. The South Carolina results also marked the end of the road for John Edwards. Soon after finishing a distant third he announced that he was suspending his campaign.

After South Carolina, the paths of the Democratic and Republican presidential candidates diverged. For Democrats, the next major test was on Super Tuesday. Because Florida, like Michigan, had been stripped of its national convention delegates by the Democratic National Committee for violating party rules by scheduling its primary before February 5, all of the major Democratic candidates had promised not to campaign in the state. For the Republican candidates, though, and especially for Rudy Giuliani, Florida loomed very large. Even though the Republican National Committee had cut the state's national convention delegation in half, Florida was still a large prize and, more importantly, the state's primary took place only one week before Super Tuesday with its treasure trove of delegates.

Florida provided John McCain with an opportunity to cement his status as the front-runner for the Republican nomination. For the other remaining Republican candidates, though, Florida was a matter of survival. Rudy Giuliani, the onetime front-runner for the Republican nomination, had staked everything on Florida, a state with a large population of émigrés from New York. After skipping Iowa, New Hampshire, and South Carolina, Giuliani desperately needed a win in the Sunshine State to convince Republican voters and contributors that he was still a viable candidate. And after three consecutive defeats, including a weak showing in South Carolina, Mitt Romney also needed a strong showing in Florida to stop his campaign's downhill slide. Finally, Florida offered Mike Huckabee a chance to demonstrate his vote-getting ability in a state with a much larger and more diverse electorate than Iowa.

In the end it was John McCain who emerged victorious in Florida, grabbing 36 percent of the vote and gaining big momentum going into Super Tuesday. Mitt Romney's second place finish, five points behind McCain, was good enough to allow him to continue his campaign for at least another week. For Rudy Giuliani, though, Florida was the end of the road. Within hours of learning that he had finished third with 15 percent of the vote, only one point ahead of Mike Huckabee, Giuliani announced his withdrawal from the Republican race. The next day he formally endorsed John McCain.

Florida, along with Michigan, was not supposed to matter in the Democratic nomination battle. Both states had been stripped of their delegates by the Democratic National Committee and all of the candidates had agreed not to campaign in either contest. But that was before Hillary Clinton realized that she was facing a very serious challenge for the Democratic nomination from Barack Obama. After scoring a big win in the state's uncontested primary, just as she had in Michigan where Obama's name was not even on the ballot, Clinton made a dramatic appearance in Florida on the night of the primary to "claim victory" and demand that all of Florida's and Michigan's delegates be seated at the Democratic convention. It was the beginning of what would turn into a bitter and protracted battle between the Clinton and Obama campaigns over the two states—a battle that would not be resolved until shortly before the party's convention.

Super Tuesday

On Tuesday, February 5, the largest number of states in the history of the presidential nominating process held primaries or caucuses on the same day. A total of 24 states held contests in one or both parties, including 16 Democratic primaries and 15 Republican primaries. When all of the results had been tabulated, the Republican Party was very close to having its nomination decided but the outlook for the Democratic nomination was more uncertain than ever.

Table 2. National Vote in Super Tuesday Primaries
(Votes in Thousands)

16 Democratic Primaries

Clinton	7,312	49.2%
Obama	7,117	47.9
Other	439	2.0
Total	14,868	100.0%

15 Republican Primaries

McCain	3,608	40.5%
Romney	2,918	32.7
Huckabee	1,781	20.0
Other	609	6.8
Total	8,916	100.0%

Source: cnnpolitics.com

The results of the Super Tuesday primaries are summarized in Table 2. Almost 24 million Americans voted in primary elections on February 5 with hundreds of thousands more taking part in party caucuses. It was by far the largest number of votes cast on a single day in the history of the presidential nominating process with many states setting turnout records. Continuing a pattern evident in earlier contests, far more voters took part in Democratic primaries than in Republican primaries.

While each of the three remaining major contenders for the Republican nomination enjoyed some victories on Super Tuesday, it was John McCain who walked away with the lion's share of the delegates to the Republican convention. By finishing first in a number of big states with winner-take-all primaries, including New York and California, McCain emerged from Super Tuesday with an almost insurmountable delegate lead over his principal rivals. Soon afterward Mitt Romney announced that he was suspending his campaign, leaving Mike Huckabee as the only remaining major challenger to John McCain and virtually assuring the Arizona senator of the GOP nomination. Huckabee would soldier on for several more weeks, winning a few primaries in southern states with large concentrations of conservative evangelicals, but he could never expand his appeal beyond that segment of the Republican base.

Many political observers had expected Super Tuesday to decide both parties' presidential nominations. It did effectively decide the Republican nomination, but on the Democratic side Super Tuesday made it clear that the race between Hillary Clinton and Barack Obama was likely to go on for some time and might not be decided until the last primaries or even the national convention. The two Democrats split the vote on Super Tuesday almost evenly and the Democratic Party's proportional allocation rules ensured that the delegates chosen in the primaries and caucuses would be almost evenly divided as well. But while the votes and delegates were almost evenly divided, it was Barack Obama who came out of Super Tuesday with momentum going into the next round of primaries and caucuses. In battling the vaunted Clinton political machine to a draw, Barack Obama had stunned many Democratic Party leaders and pundits and shattered Hillary Clinton's aura of inevitability.

The Later Primaries and Caucuses

The Super Tuesday results made it clear that the battle for the Democratic nomination would be a marathon but only one of the two campaigns was prepared to run a marathon. Hillary Clinton's campaign had apparently assumed that Super Tuesday would be the end of the Democratic nomination race. Based on this assumption, they spent almost all of their available funds on the February 5 primaries and had little left over for the next round of contests. In addition, the

Clinton campaign had done little to organize in states holding primaries and caucuses in the weeks following Super Tuesday. In contrast, the Obama campaign's strategy was based on the assumption that the nomination race would go on through the end of the Democratic primaries. They had organizations in place in all of the states holding contests in February and March, including the caucus states, which had largely been ignored by the Clinton campaign.

Meanwhile, Barack Obama was enjoying a growing financial advantage over Hillary Clinton. After matching Clinton during 2007, the Obama campaign was using its Internet fund-raising prowess to pull far ahead of Clinton during the first quarter of 2008. Between January and March, Obama outraised Clinton by 132 million dollars to 73 million dollars. By the end of March, the Obama campaign had almost 43 million dollars in cash on hand and less than one million dollars in debts while the Clinton campaign had only 8.6 million dollars in cash on hand and 10.3 million dollars in debts including a 5 million dollar loan by Hillary Clinton to her campaign. As a result, Obama was able to outspend Clinton by a wide margin in almost all of the primaries after Super Tuesday.

In a span of four weeks following Super Tuesday, Barack Obama defeated Hillary Clinton in nine consecutive primaries and caucuses, winning decisive victories in the Virginia and Maryland primaries on February 19 and the Wisconsin primary on February 26. By the time Hillary Clinton was able to bounce back with wins in the Ohio and Texas primaries on March 4, Obama had established a clear lead in elected delegates, a lead that he would never relinquish. Even on March 4, Obama was able to keep Clinton's margins small enough in Ohio and Texas to prevent her from gaining much of an advantage in the delegate count while winning the Texas caucuses that took place on the same night as the state's primary.

While he was pulling ahead of Hillary Clinton in elected delegates, Barack Obama was forced to deal with a new problem in mid-March: the appearance on the Internet of incendiary excerpts from sermons given by his former pastor, Jeremiah Wright. In these excerpts Wright, who had been a mentor to Obama during his years as a community organizer in Chicago and had presided at Obama's wedding, was harshly critical of the United States for its history of racism, using language such as "God damn the United States of America." It was potentially damaging information and the Clinton campaign was quick to exploit the opening by suggesting that Obama should have resigned his membership in Wright's church because of the content of the sermons.

Although the Obama campaign had generally avoided discussing racial issues during the campaign in order to not give the impression that Obama was running as a black candidate, the growing controversy over Wright's sermons forced Obama to respond and on March 18 he gave a lengthy televised speech on race relations from Philadelphia. In the speech Obama sought to distance himself from Wright's controversial comments, emphasizing his belief in the American dream and love of country while attempting to explain the sources of black anger in American history. The speech was generally well received by media commentators and the public and, for a while at least, the controversy appeared to die down.

Between March 4 and the end of the primary season on June 5 Obama and Clinton traded victories in a series of primaries with the end result being little change in the delegate balance. Each candidate had strong support among important blocs of Democratic voters. Obama appealed to younger and better educated whites along with African-Americans; Clinton appealed to older, less educated whites, especially older white women, and Hispanics. Throughout March, April, and May, national polls showed almost even support for Clinton and Obama among Democratic voters. Not even a new controversy over an angry speech to the National Press Club by Obama's former pastor, Jeremiah Wright, in late April could shake up the race. It was like a slugfest between two heavyweights and neither one could land a knockout blow.

The Superdelegates and the Democratic End-Game

Because of the closeness of the race, the Democratic Party's proportional allocation rules, and the fact that 15 percent of the delegate slots at the national convention were reserved for uncommitted superdelegates, neither Clinton nor Obama could win an outright majority of delegates in the primaries and caucuses. That meant that it would be the superdelegates who would ultimately choose the nominee. And despite Hillary Clinton's attempts to convince these party and elected officials that she would be a stronger candidate in November against John McCain, as the primary season came to an end, more and more superdelegates began to line up behind the candidate who had won a majority of the delegates elected in the primaries and caucuses, Barack Obama. Whatever their personal preference had been for the nomination, most of these party and elected officials did not want to be seen as overturning the decisions made by rank-and-file

Democratic voters. And so, by the end of the primaries on June 3 it was clear that Barack Obama had an insurmountable lead in the overall delegate count and a few days later Hillary Clinton suspended her campaign. The junior senator from Illinois would be the Democratic nominee against John McCain. But before the general election campaign could begin, Obama and McCain would have to choose their running mates and both parties would hold their largely symbolic but strategically important national nominating conventions.

The Vice-Presidential Selections and National Conventions

The most important decision that Barack Obama and John McCain faced between the end of the primary season and their party's national conventions was choosing a running mate. While vice-presidential candidates have rarely had a major impact on the outcomes of presidential elections, vice presidents have come to play a more and more important role as presidential advisors and confidantes in recent years. As a result, the choice of a running mate is now viewed by media commentators as the first presidential decision made by a candidate for the Oval Office and is subject to intense scrutiny.

There is no hard and fast rule about when presidential candidates announce their vice-presidential selection. Some, like John Kerry in 2004, have made their decision public well before their party's convention, some have waited until just before the convention, and some have waited until after the convention gets under way to create additional drama. Barack Obama decided to announce his choice, Delaware Senator Joseph Biden, on August 23, only two days before the opening of the Democratic convention in Denver, Colorado. Biden was viewed as a relatively safe choice—a mainstream Democrat whose years of service as ranking minority member and chair of the Senate Foreign Relations Committee would compensate for Obama's limited foreign policy experience. While Biden had a reputation for committing occasional verbal gaffes, including a controversy over plagiarizing words from a speech by a British politician during his abortive 1988 presidential campaign, the fact that he had twice been a candidate for president meant that he had already been vetted by the press. And his hardscrabble childhood and image as a strong family man were seen as appealing to white working class voters whom Obama was having some difficulty with. Most importantly, Biden was widely viewed as a credible successor if something were to happen to a President Obama.

National nominating conventions no longer choose the presidential candidates. They simply ratify the decision made by the voters in the primaries and caucuses. Nevertheless, these quadrennial gatherings still play an important role in presidential elections by providing each party with an opportunity to showcase its new nominee and kick off its general election campaign. Today's national conventions serve as four-day-long infomercials for the political parties. As such, every minute of the convention is carefully scripted with special attention to each day's prime-time speeches since those are the only parts of the convention covered by the major television networks.

From this standpoint, the 2008 Democratic convention was a rousing success. The last remaining major bone of contention between the Clinton and Obama campaigns—the treatment of the Florida and Michigan delegations—was resolved shortly before the convention began when Barack Obama asked that both states have all of their delegates seated with full voting rights. From that point on the convention proceeded according to plan with rousing prime-time speeches by Hillary and Bill Clinton as well as the new vice-presidential candidate, Joe Biden. Obama's acceptance speech, delivered in front of 80,000 wildly cheering spectators in Denver's Mile High Stadium, received rave reviews from most of the pundits and political commentators. It appeared that the Democrats were leaving Denver unified for the remainder of the campaign and polls taken immediately after the convention indicated that the message had gotten through to the party's rank-and-file. According to the Gallup tracking poll, Obama's overall lead over John McCain increased from just two or three points just before the convention to seven or eight points immediately after the convention with most of the gains occurring among self-identified Democrats.

Watching the proceedings in Denver, John McCain's campaign team knew that it was facing a major challenge. Not only was the national political environment a very difficult one for Republicans, but it now appeared that the rift between the Clinton and Obama campaigns had largely been healed and that the Democratic Party was united behind Barack Obama's candidacy. Moreover, polls showed that rank-and-file Democrats were much more enthusiastic about their party's nominee than rank-and-file Republicans were about John McCain.

Facing all of these challenges, the McCain campaign made a bold but risky decision. Rather than making a relatively safe pick for the vice-presidential nomination, someone like Minnesota Governor Tim Pawlenty, who had been rumored to be at the top of John McCain's short list of potential running mates, the McCain campaign decided to go all-in by choosing Governor Sarah Palin of Alaska. The Palin pick, announced on the morning of August 29, the day after Barack Obama's acceptance speech and three days before the opening of the Republican convention, stunned many political observers. Palin was virtually unknown outside of her home state of Alaska where she had served as governor for less than two years. Before her election as governor, Palin had been the mayor of Wasilla, Alaska, a town located on the outskirts of Anchorage with a population of less than ten thousand.

Palin was a political unknown but she seemed to have several advantages to the McCain campaign team over her better known rivals. First, there would be considerable curiosity about her, which might lead to increased media coverage and public interest in the Republican ticket; second, as a woman, she might appeal to disgruntled Hillary Clinton supporters; third, her membership in a Pentecostal church and her reputation as a staunch opponent of abortion and gay marriage might increase enthusiasm and turnout among religious conservatives who were not excited about John McCain's candidacy; and fourth, her youth, physical appearance, and photogenic family might appeal to younger voters who found it hard to warm up to a 72-year-old presidential candidate. Even the subsequent revelation that Palin's unmarried 17-year-old daughter was pregnant could be spun as a positive development—the daughter's decision to marry the teenage father and have the baby were seen as reinforcing Palin's appeal to religious conservatives.

The choice of Sarah Palin as John McCain's running mate seemed to pay immediate dividends. Palin's acceptance speech at the Republican convention drew a huge television audience—as large as those for Barack Obama's and John McCain's acceptance speeches. And Palin's folksy style and sharp attacks on the Democratic ticket received a wildly enthusiastic reception from the delegates in Minneapolis. Polls in the week following the Republican convention showed an immediate uptick in enthusiasm among GOP voters. They also showed John McCain, for the first time in several months, with a narrow lead over Barack Obama. For the moment at least, the choice of Sarah Palin seemed to be working just as the McCain campaign had hoped.

The General Election Campaign: The Money Game

Republicans had reason to feel optimistic in the immediate aftermath of what had been, by all accounts, a very successful national convention. Presidential candidates typically receive a bounce in the polls right after their party's convention but McCain's bounce was larger than most and larger than the bounce Obama had received following the Democratic convention—large enough to give him a small lead in a number of post-convention polls. Tempering the Republican's optimism, though, were two crucial facts. The national political environment remained extremely difficult for the GOP and, for the first time ever, the Democratic presidential candidate had a significant financial advantage over his Republican opponent.

Barack Obama's decision in June to turn down public financing for his general election campaign had received widespread criticism from pundits and political commentators. Obama was the first presidential candidate to turn down public financing of his general election campaign since the current system was created following the Watergate scandal in the 1970s. Some commentators thought that it was risky to turn down 84 million dollars in public funds in the hope that the campaign would be able to raise more money in private contributions. Others thought that the decision would damage Obama's image as a reformer and allow the McCain campaign to paint him as an opportunistic flip-flopper since he had earlier agreed to accept public financing. As it turned out, though, the critics were badly mistaken. While the McCain campaign tried to turn Obama's rejection of public financing into a campaign issue, these criticisms never seemed to resonate with the electorate. A Gallup poll found that voters in 2008 were much more concerned about issues that directed affected their lives such as jobs, taxes, and health care, than they were about an "inside baseball" issue like campaign finance. And by turning down public financing, the Obama campaign was able to use the sophisticated fund-raising apparatus that it had constructed for the primaries to financially overwhelm the McCain campaign.

By accepting public financing, John McCain received an infusion of 84.1 million dollars into his campaign immediately following the Republican convention. But it also meant that he could not raise additional campaign funds from private donors, and in the month of September alone, Barack Obama raised over 150 million dollars. As a result, even with substantial assistance from the

Republican National Committee, the McCain campaign found itself being badly outspent during the fall campaign.

According to data compiled by the Campaign Finance Institute, between September 1 and October 14, the Obama campaign and the Democratic National Committee outspent the McCain campaign and the Republican National Committee by 266 million dollars to 176 million dollars. Moreover, the McCain campaign was much more financially dependent on the RNC than the Obama campaign was on the DNC. Almost two-thirds of the spending on the Republican side, 111 million out of 176 million dollars, came from the Republican National Committee. In contrast, less than a quarter of the spending on the Democratic side, 64 million out of 266 million dollars, came from the Democratic National Committee. This meant that the Obama campaign had much more control than the McCain campaign over how money was spent, including the content of political advertising.

Because of its huge fund-raising advantage, the Obama campaign was able to outspend the McCain campaign on television advertising by a wide margin in almost every battleground state. In Florida, Virginia, Ohio, and Colorado, voters saw two or three times as many Obama ads as McCain ads during the final weeks of the campaign. And in the final week of the campaign, the Obama campaign was so flush with cash that it was able to purchase air time on several major networks to broadcast a 30-minute infomercial during prime time, an infomercial that was viewed by more than 30 million households across the United States. Even with efforts by some independent conservative groups to aid the Republican ticket, as Election Day approached the Obama campaign's messages were being viewed by more voters more frequently than the McCain campaign's messages.

The Campaign Messages

Given the political environment in which the 2008 election took place, it is not surprising that both campaigns emphasized messages of change during their conventions and in their subsequent political advertising. As the out-party, of course, it was natural for the Democrats to focus their message heavily on criticism of the performance of the incumbent Republican administration. At every opportunity, Barack Obama and Joe Biden sought to tie John McCain to George Bush, emphasizing the Republican standard-bearer's support for the president's policies at home and abroad, and especially his support for the administration's economic policies. McCain and Palin, on the other hand, sought to put as much distance between themselves and the unpopular occupant of the Oval Office as possible. They frequently referred to themselves as "mavericks" who had challenged the Republican establishment during their political careers and promised to bring reform to Washington if elected. Neither President Bush nor his equally unpopular vice president, Dick Cheney, ever appeared on the campaign trail with John McCain or Sarah Palin. Nor did they appear in any political ads sponsored by the McCain campaign or the Republican Party. The president and vice president were featured prominently, however, in ads sponsored by the Obama campaign and the Democratic Party.

Beyond a common emphasis on the need for change, however, there were marked differences between the advertising strategies and messages of the Obama and McCain campaigns. While both campaigns ran a wide variety of ads, and the Obama campaign ran far more ads than the McCain campaign, the proportion of negative ads was much higher on the Republican side than on the Democratic side. During the final weeks of the campaign, according to data compiled by the Wisconsin Advertising Project, the large majority of ads sponsored by the Republican Party and the McCain campaign consisted of attacks on Barack Obama's character and record, ads that sought to portray him as inexperienced in national affairs, naïve in his approach to foreign policy, and an extreme liberal on domestic issues.

In addition to portraying Obama as an extreme liberal who would raise taxes on the middle class and surrender in Iraq, Republican ads and speeches by John McCain and Sarah Palin on the campaign trail repeatedly sought to suggest that Obama had a hidden radical past by linking him with William Ayers, a onetime member of a radical anti-Vietnam War organization called the Weather Underground that had carried out a series of bombings during the 1960s and 1970s. Years later, Ayers had become a distinguished professor in the Department of Education at the University of Illinois campus in Chicago where he served on several local community boards, regularly consulted with prominent political leaders, and came to know Barack Obama. But while Obama and Ayers were acquainted, and Ayers had hosted a fund-raiser for Obama during his first campaign for the Illinois state senate, the two were never personal friends and Obama had strongly criticized Ayers's actions as a member of the Weather Underground—actions that took place when Obama was still in grade school.

The use of fear tactics has a long history in American political campaigns and they have sometimes been successful. In 2002, for example, Republican ads in the aftermath of the September 11 attacks suggested that several incumbent Democratic senators, including Vietnam War veteran and triple amputee Max Cleland of Georgia, were soft on terrorism for opposing provisions of the Patriot Act that would have reduced the job protections of federal employees. The ads juxtaposed images of the Democratic senators with an image of Osama bin Laden. Several of the Democratic incumbents, including Cleland, lost their seats. In 2008, however, the McCain campaign's attempt to link Barack Obama to Bill Ayers and the Weather Underground appeared to fall flat. Polls conducted during the final weeks of the campaign indicated that voters found the ads unpersuasive and disliked the negative tone of the McCain campaign.

Whether any political message is effective depends on the receptivity of voters to that message. That in turn depends on the mood of the public. In the fall of 2002, barely a year after the September 11 attacks, with American troops at war in Afghanistan and George W. Bush enjoying an approval rating of over 60 percent, many voters were receptive to a message suggesting that Democratic senators who opposed the president on a national security issue were soft on terrorism. In 2008, however, with the economy in crisis and President Bush's approval rating below 30 percent, far fewer voters were receptive to the McCain campaign's message that Barack Obama was an extreme liberal who enjoyed, in the words of Sarah Palin, "palling around with" domestic terrorists.

The Financial Crisis

At the beginning of the fall campaign the mood of the American public was already extremely sour. Real incomes had been falling and home foreclosures and unemployment had been rising for months. Most Americans already believed that the country was in a recession even though official government statistics had not yet confirmed that fact. And the public's mood turned even more negative after September 14. On that date it was announced that Lehman Brothers, one of Wall Street's largest and most prestigious investment banks, was declaring bankruptcy due to massive losses on its mortgage-related securities. That same day, the sale of Merrill Lynch, another Wall Street icon, to Bank of America was announced. Again, the explanation was huge losses on the firm's mortgage-related investments. Although warning signs of an impending financial crisis had been evident for months, it was the beginning of the Wall Street meltdown of 2008.

On Monday, September 15, the Dow Jones Industrial Average lost more than 500 points, or more than four percent of its value. Over the next several days, the stock market remained volatile but generally continued to spiral downward. More importantly, national and international credit markets began to seize up out of fear that other large financial institutions might fail. On September 17, AIG, one of the nation's largest insurance companies, suffered a liquidity crisis due to the declining value of its investments in the credit default swaps market. To stave off a bankruptcy that could have had disastrous consequences for the credit markets as well as for many individuals, businesses, and government agencies insured by AIG, the Federal Reserve announced a plan to provide the insurance giant with 85 billion dollars in additional credit in exchange for an ownership share in the company. It was an unprecedented move, and was especially shocking in coming from a conservative, pro-business administration. But it was only a hint of even more massive government intervention in the credit markets to come.

With little apparent improvement in the credit markets and more financial institutions teetering on the brink of bankruptcy, on Friday, September 19, Treasury Secretary Henry Paulson proposed a dramatic plan to save the nation's faltering financial institutions—a 700 billion dollar bailout plan that would have the federal government purchase toxic assets from endangered banks in order to infuse capital into the nation's financial system. It was a plan so enormous and so unprecedented that it forced an immediate reaction not only from Wall Street but from leaders in Congress and the presidential candidates.

Despite the strong endorsement of President Bush, initial reactions to the proposed bailout plan from Democratic and Republican leaders on Capitol Hill were decidedly mixed. While recognizing the severity of the crisis and the need for action, many Democrats were suspicious of any plan proposed by the Bush administration and wanted major changes to provide stronger guarantees to taxpayers and direct assistance to homeowners threatened by foreclosure before they were willing to sign on. At the same time, many Republicans found the idea of a massive federal bailout of private sector institutions antithetical to their conservative, free-market ideology. The bailout plan was clearly going to be a hard sell on Capitol Hill.

Initially both presidential candidates adopted a wait-and-see attitude toward the proposed bailout. But then the McCain campaign made a startling announcement. On Wednesday, September 24, John McCain announced that he was suspending his campaign to go back to Washington and participate in the negotiations in Congress on the bailout legislation. He also asked that the first presidential debate, which was scheduled to take place two days later in Oxford, Mississippi, be postponed until an agreement could be reached on the bailout plan.

McCain's announcement was greeted with a mixture of surprise and skepticism by most media commentators. Since the negotiations over the bailout package were already well underway in Congress, it was not clear what role, if any, Senator McCain could play in that process. In fact, even after his return to Washington there was little evidence that he was deeply involved in the discussions. Meanwhile, both the debate organizers and the Obama campaign announced that they were opposed to postponing the first presidential debate. Although no agreement had been reached on a bailout package, on Friday morning the McCain campaign announced that the Arizona Senator would take part in the debate because sufficient progress toward a compromise had been made. However, when the bailout legislation came to a vote in the House of Representatives on Monday, September 29, it went down to defeat because a large majority of Republicans voted against the bill despite Senator McCain's endorsement. It was not until ten days later, after a major decline in stock market prices and frenzied negotiations between Secretary Paulson and congressional leaders, that the Senate, and then the House, passed a revised bailout bill. Both John McCain and Barack Obama voted in favor of the revised bill in the Senate.

Passage of the bailout plan did not, of course, end the financial crisis. Over the next several weeks credit markets remained tight and stock prices continued to plummet, with key indices falling to their lowest levels in many years. Meanwhile, other economic indicators were turning even more negative than earlier in the year. In October the Commerce Department announced that the nation's gross domestic product, the total output of goods and services, had fallen by an estimated 0.3 percent during the third quarter of 2008. It was the worst GDP report in more than a decade and was widely seen as signaling that the nation was already in a recession. Then in early November, the Labor Department announced that the U.S. economy had shed more than 200,000 jobs during the month of October and that the official unemployment rate had risen to 6.5 percent, its highest level in 14 years.

The worsening condition of the nation's economy during the fall was clearly a major problem for the McCain campaign. Making the situation even worse, though, was Senator McCain's erratic behavior in the aftermath of the financial crisis and his statement in early September, before the collapse of the stock market, that the nation's economy was "fundamentally sound." The Obama campaign, of course, was quick to exploit the opening that Senator McCain provided, featuring the "fundamentally sound" comment in many of its campaign speeches and advertisements and using the financial crisis to link John McCain to the failed economic policies of the Bush administration. Meanwhile, Senator Obama himself, by remaining above the fray during the negotiations over the bailout package and then endorsing the final product, was able to appear calm and "presidential" in contrast to Senator McCain, who appeared to adopt a new strategy every 24 hours. By mid-September, the lead that John McCain had briefly enjoyed in the polls following the Republican convention had evaporated and by the end of the month Barack Obama had established a clear advantage in the national polls and in most of the battleground states. It was an advantage he would never relinquish. Between September 26 and Election Day, John McCain never led Barack Obama in a single national poll.

The Presidential and Vice-Presidential Debates

Although the first televised debate between presidential candidates took place in 1960 between Richard Nixon and John F. Kennedy, debates have only been a regular feature of these contests since 1976 with the first vice-presidential debate taking place in 1984 between George H. W. Bush and Geraldine Ferraro. Every presidential campaign since 1992 has included three presidential debates and a single vice-presidential debate. While these events are often eagerly anticipated by the media, and the presidential and vice-presidential candidates devote a great deal of time and effort to preparing for them, their effects on the presidential race are typically fairly small. That is because by the time the debates take place, most voters already have their minds made up and those supporting a candidate rarely change their mind as a result of watching a debate. In addition, presidential and vice-presidential candidates are generally skilled at answering the questions they want to answer during a debate, regardless of what questions they are asked. As a result, major gaffes are rare.

    The 2008 presidential and vice-presidential debates were no exception to these rules. Although the formats of the debates and the subjects discussed in them varied, the results were very similar. Polls taken immediately after all three presidential debates and the single vice-presidential debate found that the Democratic candidates, Barack Obama and Joe Biden, had bested the Republican candidates, John McCain and Sarah Palin. One interesting sidelight to these debates, though, was that for the first time the audience for the vice-presidential debate was larger than the audience for any of the presidential debates. Apparently many members of the public were eager to see how Sarah Palin would do in the vice-presidential debate in the aftermath of her widely criticized interview with CBS news anchor Katie Couric. Most media commentators felt that Palin performed well in the debate, avoiding any mistakes and displaying the folksy charm that she had used so effectively in her acceptance speech at the Republican convention. Nevertheless, according to the polls, most viewers of the debate rated Joe Biden as the winner.

    The third presidential debate was also notable for John McCain's repeated references to an Ohio plumber named Joe Wurzelbacher to illustrate his criticisms of Barack Obama's tax proposals. McCain claimed that "Joe the Plumber" was upset about Obama's plan to "redistribute the wealth" by raising taxes on Americans earning more than $250,000 a year. Obama countered that far more Americans would benefit from his proposal to cut taxes on low-to-moderate income taxpayers than from McCain's proposal to continue the Bush tax cuts. The debate may not have changed many voters' minds, but "Joe the Plumber" quickly became a fixture in campaign speeches by John McCain and Sarah Palin, and Joe himself actually appeared at several McCain campaign events.

    While the debates produced no major shifts in the polls, they may have helped to cement support for Barack Obama among some swing voters. The debates allowed Obama to go head-to-head with the much more experienced McCain on a wide range of issues, including foreign policy and national security. By simply holding his own on national security and foreign policy issues, Obama may have helped to ease some voters' concerns about his lack of experience and reduced McCain's advantage on these issues. At the same time, the debates may have reinforced Obama's advantage on domestic issues and especially on the economy. After the debates, polls generally found that his advantage over McCain on these issues was somewhat larger than before the debates.

The Ground Game

Modern political campaigns are not just about media and message. They are also about mobilization and in this area as well, the Obama campaign had a decided advantage over the McCain campaign. In 2004, both parties poured resources into registering and turning out voters in the swing states and the result was a dramatic increase in turnout. But in the end it was the Republicans who triumphed in the key battlegrounds of Florida and Ohio by putting the 72-hour program that had been developed by Karl Rove into effect. This involved using individuals identified as Bush supporters to turn out their friends and neighbors through the most effective form of voter mobilization, personal contact. The result was that while Democratic turnout increased, Republican turnout increased even more. In 2008, the Obama campaign was determined not to let that happen again.

The Obama campaign had two crucial advantages over the McCain campaign when it came to voter mobilization: money and enthusiasm. It put both of these advantages to good use. Because of the enormous success of its fund-raising operation, the Obama campaign was able to open dozens of field offices and send hundreds of paid organizers into every one of the major battleground states including Florida, Ohio, Pennsylvania, Virginia, Indiana, and North Carolina. The size of the Obama field operation was unprecedented in the history of modern political campaigns. In most of the battleground states the number of Obama field offices greatly exceeded the number of McCain field offices. According to a count by Nate Silver of fivethirtyeight.com, as of August 9 the Obama campaign had opened 336 field offices in battleground states compared with 101 for the McCain campaign, and unlike the Obama offices, many of the McCain field offices were actually being staffed by local Republican Party organizations. Obama field offices outnumbered McCain field offices by 33 to 9 in Ohio, 28 to 6 in Virginia, 27 to 7 in Missouri, and 14 to 3 in New Hampshire. In fact Florida was the only state where McCain field offices (35) outnumbered Obama field offices (25).

The other major advantage that the Obama campaign enjoyed when it came to voter mobilization was the much greater level of enthusiasm among Obama's supporters. This allowed the campaign to leverage its investment in campaign offices and paid staffers into an army of volunteers who could conduct voter registration and get-out-the-vote drives. Preliminary evidence indicates that this advantage in manpower allowed the Obama campaign to contact a larger proportion of the electorate than the McCain campaign in many of the key battleground states. According to data from state exit polls compiled by Nate Silver, the percentage of voters reporting contact by the Obama campaign exceeded the proportion reporting contact by the McCain campaign in 11 of 12 battleground states. The largest gap was in Nevada, where 50 percent of voters reported contact by the Obama campaign vs. 29 percent who reported contact by the McCain campaign. There were also double-digit contact gaps in favor of Obama in Colorado, Indiana, Virginia, Pennsylvania, and Iowa and smaller gaps in favor of Obama in Florida, North Carolina, Missouri, Ohio, and Wisconsin. The only state where more voters reported contact by the McCain campaign was West Virginia where there was a two point gap in favor of the Republican candidate. But most political observers never considered West Virginia to be a battleground state in 2008.

The Race to the Finish Line

During the last frantic days of the campaign, as the presidential and vice-presidential candidates crisscrossed the country in search of votes, it was apparent to most observers that the Democratic ticket was in a much stronger position than the Republican ticket when it came to securing the 270 votes needed to win a majority in the Electoral College. Not only did the Obama-Biden ticket lead the McCain-Palin ticket by an average margin of between 6 and 8 points in the national polls, but they also held clear leads in all 19 states that John Kerry had carried in 2004 and at least five states that George Bush had carried in that election: Iowa, New Mexico, Colorado, Virginia, and Ohio. Several other Bush states, including Florida, North Carolina, Missouri, Nevada, and Indiana were also clearly in play. Starting with a secure base of 252 electoral votes that John Kerry had won in 2004, all the Obama campaign needed to do was add one large state such as Ohio or Florida, or two medium-sized states such as Virginia and North Carolina, to get to 270.

With polls indicating that Virginia, Colorado, and Ohio were tilting toward Obama, the McCain campaign decided that their only hope of winning the election was to turn around at least one large state that had supported John Kerry in 2004 and hope that one or more of the Bush states that were leaning toward Obama would return in the end to the Republican fold. Based on their internal polling and despite numerous published polls showing Barack Obama with a comfortable lead, the blue state the McCain campaign chose to make its last stand in was Pennsylvania. And so in the final week of the campaign, both John McCain and Sarah Palin devoted several days to campaigning in Pennsylvania despite polls showing a narrower Obama margin in several other large states including Florida and Ohio. It was a decision that puzzled many outside observers. On Election Day, Barack Obama carried Pennsylvania by a margin of 10 points.

The Results

At precisely 11 P.M. Eastern Standard Time on November 4, just as the polls closed in California, Oregon, and Washington, all of the major networks declared Barack Obama to be the winner of the 2008 presidential election. After more than a year of campaigning it took only a few hours of vote counting to determine that Obama would have the 270 electoral votes that he needed to become the 44th president of the United States. In fact, he would eventually receive 365 electoral votes, the largest total since Bill Clinton in 1996.

Obama's margin in the national popular vote was more than 8.5 million, which was also the largest since Clinton's reelection victory in 1996. More than 67 million Americans cast their ballots for Barack Obama, compared with over 58 million for John McCain and almost 2 million for minor party candidates. The Democratic ticket won approximately 53 percent of the vote to approximately 46 percent for the Republican ticket and just over one percent for minor party candidates. By the standards of postwar presidential elections it was a decisive win but certainly not a landslide. The total number of votes cast for the Obama-Biden ticket was a record, however. Obama was the first Democratic presidential candidate since Jimmy Carter to win a majority of the popular vote, and Obama's 53 percent share of the popular vote was the largest for any presidential candidate since George H. W. Bush in 1988 and the largest for any Democratic candidate since Lyndon Johnson in 1964.

ELECTORAL COLLEGE VOTES IN THE 2008 ELECTION

THE UNITED STATES
A political map showing the number of electoral votes per state

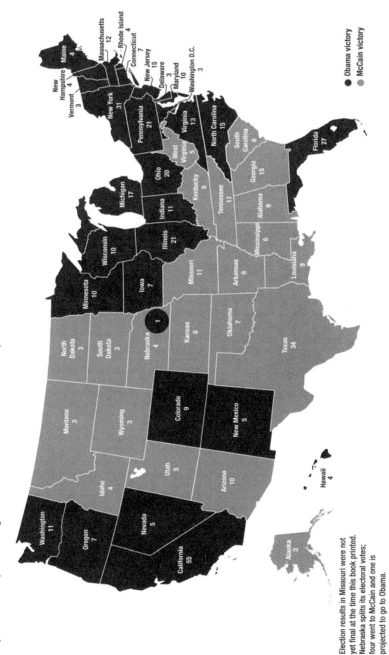

Democrats scored major gains in the congressional elections as well, picking up at least 7 seats in the Senate and at least 20 seats in the House of Representatives. It marked the second consecutive election in which Democrats made significant gains in the House and Senate. In the 2006 midterm elections they had picked up 6 Senate seats and 30 House seats. When the new Congress convened in January of 2009, Democrats would hold at least 56 seats in the Senate, even without counting Joe Lieberman, and at least 256 seats in the House, both the largest Democratic totals since the 1994 midterm election.

A glance at the 2008 electoral map on the previous page demonstrates the breadth of the Democratic sweep across the nation. The Obama-Biden ticket carried 28 states and the District of Columbia, including all 19 states won by John Kerry in 2004 and 9 states won by George W. Bush in that election. The 9 Bush states that switched to Obama were Florida, Ohio, Virginia, North Carolina, Indiana, Iowa, New Mexico, Colorado, and Nevada. Obama and Biden carried seven of the eight most populous states: California, New York, Florida, Illinois, Pennsylvania, Ohio, and Michigan. Among the most populous states, only President Bush's home state of Texas voted for John McCain. Obama's total of 365 electoral votes came to just over two-thirds of the total number of 538 and included one electoral vote from the state of Nebraska. Nebraska is one of only two states, along with Maine, that awards its electoral votes based on congressional district results. Since the Obama-Biden ticket carried one of the state's three House districts, the one that includes the city of Omaha, it received one of the state's five electoral votes. The McCain-Palin ticket received the other four electoral votes from Nebraska—two for carrying the state and one for each of the two remaining House districts.

While Barack Obama's margin in the national popular vote would not be considered a landslide, the Democratic ticket did carry many individual states by landslide or near-landslide margins, including several of the most populous states. For example, Obama carried California by 24 points, New York by 25 points, Illinois by 25 points, Michigan by 16 points, and Pennsylvania by 10 points. Of the 29 states carried by the Democratic ticket, the margin was greater than 10 points in 22 states and less than 5 points in only 4 states. And despite the decisive Democratic victory, many individual states that voted for the Republican ticket also did so by landslide or near-landslide margins. Of the 21 states carried by John McCain, the margin was greater than 10 points in 15 states and less than

5 points in only 2 states. And while the nation as a whole was moving in a Democratic direction between 2004 and 2008, the Republicans managed to increase their margin of victory in four states: Oklahoma, Arkansas, Louisiana, and Tennessee.

A similar pattern was evident in the election results at the county level. According to an analysis by the *New York Times*, between 2004 and 2008 the Democratic share of the vote increased in 2,437 of the nation's 3,141 counties; at the same time, however, the Republican share of the vote increased in 678 counties. The Democratic share of the vote increased by more than 10 points in 1,173 counties; however, the Republican share of the vote increased by more than 10 points in 225 counties. Counties with the largest increases in the Democratic share of the vote were generally found in large metropolitan areas with relatively high levels of education and large concentrations of Hispanic and African-American voters. Counties with the largest increases in the Republican share of the vote were generally found in small towns and rural areas with relatively low levels of education, small minority populations and high concentrations of Southern Baptists. Many of these Republican-tilting counties were located in the Appalachian region.

The overall picture that emerges from an examination of the 2008 electoral map is one of a country that had moved rather dramatically in a Democratic direction since 2004 but that remained deeply divided. Across all 50 states and the District of Columbia, the average margin of victory for the winning party increased from 15.8 points in 2004 to 17.4 points in 2008. There were more landslide and near-landslide states and fewer closely contested states. The number of states in which the winning candidate's margin of victory was greater than 10 points increased from 30 to 37, while the number in which the winning candidate's margin of victory was less than 5 points decreased from 11 to 6. Of the seven most populous states, only two—Florida and Ohio—were decided by less than 5 points while three—New York, California, and Illinois—were decided by more than 20 points.

Although Barack Obama won a decisive victory in 2008, there was wide divergence in his support across states and regions of the country. This pattern of geographical polarization is consistent with the pattern evident in other recent presidential elections, including the 2004 election, but it represents a dramatic change from the more homogeneous voting patterns that existed during the 1960s and 1970s. In the closely contested 1960 and 1976 elections, for example, there were far more closely contested states and far fewer landslide states than in recent presidential elections. And in both of those elections every one of the most populous states was closely contested, including California, New York, Illinois and Texas. The divisions between red states and blue states are far deeper today than they were 30 or 40 years ago and the 2008 election did nothing to change that reality.

Further evidence of shifting voting patterns can be seen in the results of the 2004 and 2008 national exit polls. Barack Obama did substantially better than John Kerry among most groups of voters, including men and women, college graduates and non-graduates, and lower- and upper-income voters. However, the size of Democratic gains between 2004 and 2008 varied considerably based on two characteristics—age and race. Obama's gains were much greater among younger voters than among older voters. According to the exit poll data, Obama carried voters under the age of 30 by a margin of 34 points vs. only 9 points for Kerry. However, he did slightly worse than Kerry among voters over the age of 65, losing that group by 8 points vs. 6 points for Kerry. As a result, the generation gap in candidate preference was much greater in 2008 than in 2004.

Obama also made much larger gains among African-American and Hispanic voters than among white voters. In addition to increasing African-American turnout, Obama also won the African-American vote by a much larger margin than John Kerry—91 points vs. 77 points. However, the most dramatic improvement in Democratic performance between 2004 and 2008 occurred among Hispanic voters. According to the exit poll data, Obama won the Hispanic vote by 36 points vs. Kerry's margin of only 10 points. In contrast, the improvement in Democratic performance among white voters was much smaller. Obama lost the white vote by a margin of 12 points vs. 17 points for John Kerry.

No Democratic presidential candidate since Lyndon Johnson has won a majority of the white vote, so the fact that Barack Obama lost the white vote was hardly surprising. In fact, Obama's 12 point deficit among white voters was identical to that of Al Gore in 2000. However, the fact that white voters favored the Republican presidential candidate by a double-digit margin in 2008 despite the poor condition of the economy and the extraordinary unpopularity of the incumbent Republican president suggests that racial prejudice did have an impact on the level of white support for the Democratic candidate.

Further evidence of the effects of race can be seen in state exit poll results. White support for Barack Obama varied dramatically across regions and states, ranging from a low of around 10 percent in the Deep South to close to 60 percent in parts of the Northeast and West. In many states outside the South, Obama did substantially better than Kerry among white voters. Between 2004 and 2008 the Democratic share of the white vote increased by 5 points in California and Washington, 7 points in Michigan and Wisconsin, 8 points in Colorado, and 9 points in Oregon. In many southern and border states, however, Obama did no better or worse than Kerry among white voters. Between 2004 and 2008 the Democratic share of the white vote fell by 4 points in Mississippi, 6 points in Arkansas, 9 points in Alabama, and 10 points in Louisiana. Based on these results, it is hard to avoid the conclusion that racial prejudice was a factor in limiting support for Barack Obama among white voters in the southern and border states. But this was not enough to cost Obama the election because his losses among these groups of white voters were offset by gains among white voters in other parts of the country, especially among younger white voters, and by increased turnout and support among African-American and Hispanic voters.

It is impossible to know whether a white candidate like Hillary Clinton would have won the election by a bigger margin than Obama. Clinton might have run somewhat stronger than Obama among older, less-educated white voters and she probably would have won a larger share of the vote in southern and border states such as Arkansas, Kentucky, and West Virginia; but Clinton might not have run as strongly as Obama among younger and better-educated white voters, and she almost certainly would not have generated the level of turnout and support among African-American voters that Obama did—turnout and support that was crucial in producing Democratic victories in states such as Virginia and North Carolina. One question can be answered definitely, however, based on the national exit poll results. Speculation that large numbers of Democrats who supported Hillary Clinton during the primaries would defect to John McCain in November proved to be groundless. Thanks in part to strong support from Hillary and Bill Clinton during the fall campaign, 85 percent of these Clinton Democrats voted for Barack Obama.

Explaining Obama's Victory

The decisive Democratic victory in the 2008 presidential election can best be understood as a product of three distinct sets of factors: changes in the composition of the American electorate, some of which had been developing for decades and some of which were more recent in origin; short-term forces at work in 2008, including the unpopularity of President Bush and the dire condition of the U.S. economy; and the campaigns conducted by the Democratic and Republican candidates. Economic conditions and the actions of the presidential and vice-presidential candidates received extensive coverage in the media during the campaign, but far less attention was paid to shifts in the composition of the electorate. However, Barack Obama's election would not have been possible without these changes.

Perhaps the most important long-term trend in the composition of the American electorate has been a gradual increase in the proportion of nonwhite voters. This trend has been occurring for at least 50 years and it is likely to continue for the foreseeable future based on Census Bureau projections of the racial and ethnic makeup of the American population between now and 2050. It has been a result of increased immigration from Asia, Africa and Latin America, higher birth rates among minority groups, and increased registration and turnout among African-Americans, Hispanics, and other nonwhite citizens.

According to data from the American National Election Studies, between 1956 and 2004 the nonwhite share of the U.S. electorate increased dramatically, going from less than one in twenty voters in 1956 to close to one in four voters in 2004. This trend continued in 2008, helped in part by an aggressive Democratic registration and get-out-the-vote campaign in African-American and Hispanic communities. National exit poll data show that the nonwhite share of the electorate increased from 23 percent in 2004 to 26 percent in 2008 with African-Americans going from 11 percent of the electorate in 2004 to 13 percent in 2008.

Since the 1970s the composition of the nonwhite electorate has itself been changing, with Hispanics (who are included here in the nonwhite population although they can be of any race) and Asian-Americans comprising a growing share of nonwhite voters. Both of these groups continue to be underrepresented in the electorate relative to their numbers in the voting-age population due to high rates of noncitizenship and relatively low registration and turnout rates. However, both groups are growing rapidly. Hispanics are now the largest minority group in the U.S. population and their share of the electorate has been rising steadily, reaching 8 percent in 2004 and 9 percent in 2008.

The growth of the nonwhite electorate, beginning with African-Americans in the 1960s and 1970s and continuing with Hispanics and Asian-Americans since the 1980s, has had profound consequences for the party system and the electoral process in the United States. African-American and Hispanic voters now comprise a large proportion of the electoral base of the Democratic Party in much of the country. The expansion of the African-American electorate made Barack Obama's nomination possible, as they provided him with a large proportion of his support in many of the Democratic primaries, especially in the South. The growth of the nonwhite electorate as a whole made Barack Obama's election possible, as African-American and other nonwhite voters provided him with a large enough margin to offset a substantial deficit among white voters.

Two related trends of more recent origin also made significant contributions to Barack Obama's victory in 2008—generational change and growing Democratic identification within the electorate. Americans under the age of 30 are now substantially more likely to identify with the Democratic Party, vote for Democratic candidates, and express liberal views on a wide range of issues than their elders. This trend was already evident in 2004 when voters under the age of 30 were the only age group to support John Kerry over George Bush, favoring the Democratic challenger by a margin of 9 points. Two years later, in the 2006 midterm elections, 18–29 year-olds supported Democratic House and Senate candidates over Republicans by better than a 20 point margin. Although younger voters were not solely responsible for the Democrats' victory, they made a significant contribution to their gains in the House and Senate. Two years later, voters under the age of 30 made an even more substantial contribution to Barack Obama's victory, turning out in large numbers (18–29 year-olds comprised 18 percent of the electorate vs. 17 percent in 2004) and supporting Obama by a 2 to 1 margin over John McCain.

Increased minority turnout and generational change contributed to another significant shift in the composition of the electorate between 2004 and 2008—increased Democratic identification. According the data from the national exit polls, voter identification with the Democratic Party increased from 35 percent in 2004 to 37 percent in 2008 while identification with the Republican Party fell from 37 percent in 2004 to 32 percent in 2008. Thus, over these four years the two parties went from parity in voter support to a seven point Democratic advantage. While this may not appear to be a dramatic change, it was highly significant because the level of party loyalty among voters has been very high in recent elections, and 2008 was no exception. According to the national exit poll, about 90 percent of Democratic and Republican identifiers voted for their party's candidate in the presidential election. Because Democrats outnumbered Republicans, however, Barack Obama had a five point lead among all party identifiers, which accounted for about two-thirds of his overall margin of victory.

Democratic gains in party identification as well as the Democratic victories in the 2008 presidential and congressional elections all reflected the dramatic changes in the political climate in the United States since the 2004 presidential election. Those changes can be clearly seen in the results of the national exit polls. Between 2004 and 2008, the proportion of voters approving of President Bush's job performance fell from 53 percent to 27 percent, while the proportion disapproving of his performance rose from 46 percent to 71 percent; the proportion of voters describing their family's financial situation as better than a year earlier fell from 32 percent to 24 percent, while the proportion describing it as worse rose from 28 percent to 42 percent; and the proportion of voters rating the national economy as excellent or good fell from 47 percent to 7 percent, while the proportion rating it as not so good or poor rose from 52 percent to 93 percent.

Such a toxic political environment would have been very difficult for any candidate from the incumbent party to overcome, even with a perfect campaign. As it was, the McCain campaign, in addition to finding itself outorganized and outspent, had great difficulty coming up with an appealing message. With a collapsing economy and a president with one of the lowest approval ratings of any chief executive in the past half century, John McCain clearly could not run on the record of the Bush administration. But despite his history of challenging the Republican establishment, McCain's attempt to position himself as a candidate of change had only limited success. In the national exit poll, half of voters thought that McCain would continue President Bush's policies, while half thought he would take the country in a different direction. Among voters who thought that he would continue Bush's policies, McCain lost to Obama by a margin of 90 percent to 8 percent. Many voters also found the tone of the McCain campaign to be overly negative. McCain's and Palin's frequent references to Obama's relationship with former Weather Underground member Bill Ayers and their attempts to suggest that Obama was concealing a radical past appeared to fall flat. In the national exit poll, 64 percent of voters indicated that the McCain campaign had attacked Barrack Obama unfairly, while only 49 percent indicated that the Obama campaign had attacked John McCain unfairly.

One final problem for John McCain was that after the initially positive response of voters to his choice of Sarah Palin as his running mate, opinions about the Alaska governor had turned increasingly negative in response to her performance in the Katie Couric interview, controversies over large expenditures on her makeup and wardrobe, and an ongoing investigation into the role that she and her husband had played in the firing of a state trooper who had been involved in a messy divorce with Palin's sister. While she remained wildly popular among GOP activists and religious conservatives and continued to draw large and enthusiastic crowds on the campaign trail, by Election Day, according to the national exit poll, only 38 percent of voters viewed her as qualified to serve as president, compared with 66 percent who viewed Joe Biden as qualified. By picking Palin as his running mate John McCain may have energized the Republican base but he may have also alienated many independent and moderate voters whose support he desperately needed.

Toward the Future

In the aftermath of the 2008 election the Democratic Party finds itself in its strongest position in government since the early 1990s. In 2009 Democrats will control the White House and both houses of Congress and their majorities in the Senate and House of Representatives will be the largest for either party since the 1994 midterm election. But President Obama and the Democratic leadership of the House and Senate will be presiding over a nation facing immense challenges at home and overseas, including a failing domestic economy, a global financial crisis, and two wars with no end in sight. And with their expanded majorities in Congress, the Democrats will have to deal with greater regional and ideological diversity in their ranks. Many of the Democrats elected to the House and Senate in 2006 and 2008 are moderates who represent districts and states with a history, until recently, of supporting Republican presidential candidates. Keeping their expanded majorities united behind President Obama's legislative program will be a difficult assignment for Speaker Pelosi and Majority Leader Reed. And in the Senate, lacking 60 votes to cut off debate, Democrats will still face the threat of Republican filibusters unless they can win over a few of the handful of remaining Republican moderates.

The Republican Party today faces the opposite problem from the Democrats. With their numbers greatly reduced by the results of the 2006 and

2008 elections, Republicans in Congress are left with a shrunken and overwhelmingly conservative party. The large majority of those who remain represent safe Republican districts and states, many in the South. There are almost no moderate Republicans left in either chamber, and the party has been decimated in the Northeast, where it now holds only a handful of House seats and only 3 of 22 Senate seats.

The GOP's electoral base has also been shrinking. Its voters are overwhelmingly white, socially conservative, middle-aged or older, and located in small towns and rural areas. In a country that is becoming increasingly urban, nonwhite and socially tolerant, that is not a good position to be in. The party's weakness among younger Americans, who not only voted for Barack Obama over John McCain by a 2 to 1 margin but who also increasingly identify with the Democratic Party, should be especially concerning to Republican strategists since research shows that once voters form an attachment to a political party they tend to maintain that attachment throughout their lives. In order to revive their fortunes, Republicans will need to find a way to reach beyond their current base—to appeal to nonwhites, young people, and an increasingly educated and socially moderate electorate.

None of this should be taken to mean that 2008 was a realigning election and that the Democratic Party will now dominate American politics for many years to come. History teaches us that winning a decisive election victory is no guarantee of future success for a political party. In 1964 the Democratic Party won an even bigger victory in the presidential and congressional elections—a victory that allowed President Lyndon Johnson to push an ambitious legislative program through Congress, including civil rights legislation, federal aid to education, the war on poverty, and Medicare. Stories in the media about the demise of the Republican Party were rampant. But two years later, with the country deeply divided over the Vietnam War, racial unrest, and a growing youth culture, Democrats suffered major setbacks in the midterm elections, and in 1968 Richard Nixon defeated Hubert Humphrey to reclaim the White House for the Republicans. Whether the Democrats will be able to consolidate the gains that they have made since 2006 is very much an open question. The answer to that question will depend largely on how they govern over the next two to four years and how the results that they produce are viewed by the American people.